Grapes

Trace Taylor

This is a grape.

Grapes come like this.

All of these are fruit.

Grapes are fruit, too.

All of these are grapes.
All grapes are not the same.

These are red grapes.

These are green grapes.

These are black grapes.

Lots of animals like to eat grapes.
Birds will eat grapes.

Skunks will eat them.

Rabbits and foxes will eat them.

People eat grapes, too.

These are grape seeds.
Many grapes have seeds in them.

We put the grape seeds in
the ground.

This is a grape vine.
Grape vines grow from the seeds.

The vines will grow big
and make lots of grapes.

We get the grapes like this.

We make juice with the grapes.

We make jelly with the juice.

We make lots of foods with grape juice.

21

These are raisins.

Raisins come from grapes, too.

Grapes are good.

They are so good that we
like to eat them like this.

Where Grapes Are Grown

Top Five Grape Producing Nations

1. China
2. Italy
3. United States
4. Spain
5. France

How Grape Juice Is Made

1. destem

2. wash

3. mash

4. cook

5. strain

6. cool

7. drink & enjoy

2G Power Words

How many can you read?

a	eat	like	red	this
all	from	lots	so	to
and	get	make	that	too
animal	good	many	the	we
are	green	not	them	will
big	have	of	these	with
black	in	people	they	
come	is	put		